finding out about BIRDS

By GENE DARBY
Supervisor and Teacher
Redding, California

Benefic Press • Westchester, Illinois

finding out about

Living Things
finding out about ANIMALS
finding out about PLANTS
finding out about BIRDS
finding out about FISH

Matter and Energy
finding out about SOLIDS, LIQUIDS, AND GASES
finding out about SIMPLE MACHINES
finding out about WEATHER
finding out about MAGNETS

Earth and the Universe
finding out about SEASONS
finding out about THE EARTH
finding out about THE SUN AND MOON
finding out about ECOLOGY

Filmstrips, Cassette, and Experiment Cards
available for each title

Library of Congress
Number 73-86783
ISBN 0-8175-7412-3

CONTENTS

Birds are animals.
Some birds are small. Some are big.

Birds of almost every color can be found.

There are many kinds of birds, but birds are all the same in some ways.

Do you know how birds are the same?

You can see birds almost every day.

How many kinds of birds do you know?

Do you know how birds build homes?

Do you know how birds get their food?

Do you know why birds can fly?

You can find out about birds.

5

WHAT IS A BIRD?

A bird is an animal.
A bird has feathers on its body.
A bird has wings.
This bird can fly with its wings.
All birds have wings, but not all birds fly.

A bird is like you in some ways.

A bird has two eyes, two legs, two ears, and two feet.

A bird is different from you in many ways.

A bird has wings instead of arms.

A bird has feathers instead of hair.

A bird has a beak and a tail.

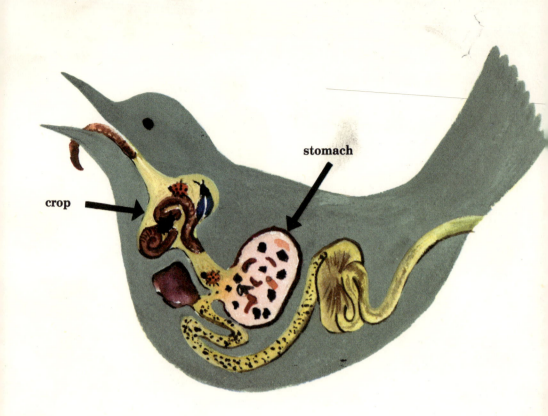

crop

stomach

Birds have
tongues, but they
have no teeth.

Some birds have a
crop which helps
grind up hard seeds
before they go to the
bird's stomach.

Birds have two eyes.

On most birds the eyes are on the sides of their heads.

A bird can see two things at once.

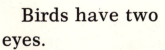

A bird must turn its head to see things in front of it.

A bird has three eyelids.
One eyelid moves up.
One moves down.
The third eyelid moves
across the eye and helps the
bird see in the sunshine.

A bird has two ears.
Its ears are on the sides of
its head, behind each eye.

ear

robin

A bird uses its beak to pick up things to eat.

It picks up many other things, too.

This bird has a different kind of beak.

This bird can get fish to eat with its beak.

great blue heron

This bird makes a hole with its beak.

It looks for food in the hole.

woodpecker

This bird uses its beak to find food in the water.

roseate spoonbill

11

Most birds have four strong toes on each foot.

perching

Birds use their toes for many things.

climbing

hunting

wading

Which foot do you think is best for
            wading
            swimming
            climbing
            perching on branches
            getting food?

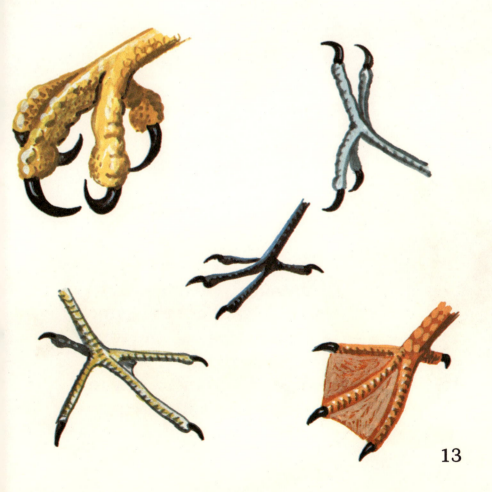

Birds are warm-blooded
animals. This means they
will stay about the same
temperature all the time.
  Birds must eat a great
deal of food every day to
keep warm and to help them
move fast.

In the winter, birds are not cold. Their feathers keep their body warm.

In the summer, birds can get too warm when they move very fast in the hot sun. Then the birds must have some way to keep cool.

Inside the bird's body are little sacs, which are like little balloons. When the bird breathes, air moves through the lungs and into these sacs to cool the bird.

FEATHERS

All birds have feathers.
Most birds have three kinds of feathers.
These feathers help birds in different ways.

There is this kind of
feather. It helps keep
the bird warm.

filoplume

This feather is very soft.
It is called down. Down feathers help birds
keep warm and dry.
Water birds have many down feathers.

down feather

contour feather

This kind of feather is harder than the other feathers are.

Feathers like this give the bird its coloring.

The biggest feathers like this are on the wings and on the tail.

They help the bird fly.

See these feathers.

See the many sizes and shapes.

golden pheasant

pheasant

red-shouldered hawk

duck wing

The colors of feathers help some birds.
The colors can look much like places where these birds live.
Birds can hide in these places.

bittern

18

These birds have bodies much the same.
Their feathers have many different colors and shapes.
Their feathers make them look different from each other.

robin

brown thrasher

bluejay

cardinal

kingfisher

19

northern gannet

blue-footed booby

These birds have oil on their feathers.
They can stay on the water in storms.
They can sleep on the water.
The water cannot get through the oil on
their feathers.

20

Find out how feathers help keep birds warm and dry.
You will need these.

Put warm water in two jars. Write down how warm the water is. Wrap one jar in a feather pillow.

Wait 15 minutes. See how warm the water is in each jar. Look at the water again in an hour. Which jar kept the water warm? Why?

Cut two pieces of paper. Tie strings around them. Tie them to a straw and balance them.

Put oil on one piece and put both pieces in water. Balance the pieces again. How is the oil on feathers good for a bird?

NESTS

Birds build many kinds of nests.
Some nests are built in trees or bushes.
Some birds build their nests on the ground.
Each bird makes its own kind of nest.

burrowing owl

bald eagle

robin

tailorbird

woodpecker

barnswallow

oriole

flamingo

23

This is a father bird.

This is a mother bird.
She is not as colorful as
the father bird.

24

The mother and father
bird must have a home.
Their home is a nest.

The mother bird works to
make the nest.
Sometimes the father bird
helps, but most of the time
he sits in the tree.
He sings to tell the other
birds that this is his place.
Others must stay away.

The mother bird uses her
feet to shape the nest.
She pats the nest into
shape with her feet.

The nest must be strong.
The mother bird looks for
mud. She picks up some
with her beak.
She uses it to make her
nest strong.

The mother bird shapes
her nest this way, too.

The mother bird
can use grass in her
nest.

BABY BIRDS

The time has come for the
mother bird to lay her eggs.
   She will lay them inside
the nest.
   There may be four or five.

Baby birds will grow inside the eggs.
   If the eggs get cold, there will be no baby
birds, so the mother bird sits on the eggs.
   She keeps them warm.
   Sometimes the father bird sits, too.

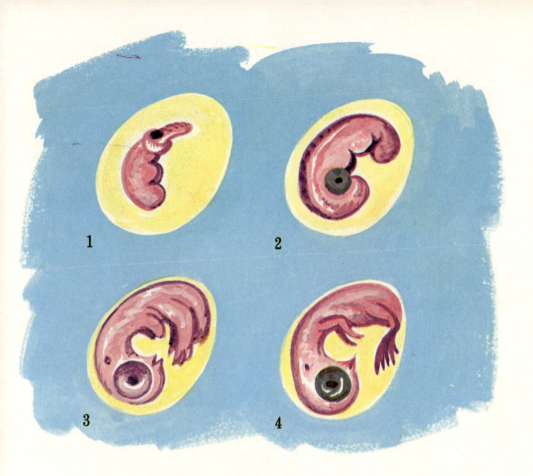

Inside the eggs, the baby birds grow.

The baby birds will come out of the eggs in about two weeks.

The baby birds are ready to come out.
The mother bird hears a pecking noise.
She looks at the egg.
One baby bird has made a hole.

The baby bird opens the egg with its egg tooth.

The tooth is on its beak. When the hole is big, the baby will come out.

At first, the baby bird is wet. The egg tooth soon falls off. The bird has no use for it now.

Now there is more pecking. All the eggs will be open soon. All the babies will soon be out.

Sometimes the mother bird finds food for
the babies.

Other times the father bird finds food for
the babies.

The babies open their eyes.
They begin to grow feathers.
They will look like their mother and father.

33

One of the baby birds is
moving about in the nest.
It stretches its wings.
It wants to fly.

The mother bird has
something good to eat.
    She holds it so the baby
bird can see.
    Soon the baby bird wants
the food.
    The baby bird is ready to
try its wings.

The baby bird pushes with its legs.
It pushes itself up in the air.

Its wings begin to open.

The baby bird pulls up its legs.

The bird's wings go up.

The bird's wings go down.

The baby bird flies!

HOW BIRDS FLY

How can birds fly?
Most birds' bodies are
shaped like this.
This shape helps the bird
fly fast.
The air slides over the
bird's body.

You can see how this
shape helps the bird fly.

Feathers help
birds to fly.
When the wings
move up, the
feathers open and
let air through.

When the wings
move down, the
feathers come closer together.
The air cannot get through.
The feathers push against the air.

When a bird does
not move its wings,
the feathers lie flat
and the air slides
over them.

38

A bird's bones help
it fly, too.

Most wing bones
are filled with air.

This helps make
the bird light enough
to fly.

muscles

The bird has strong muscles in its body.
The muscles help the bird fly.
These strong muscles move the wings up
and down.

40

Find out what things help birds fly.

You will need these.

Cut out a circle, a square, a triangle, and a V-shape. Color one side. Drop each one. How does a bird's shape help it fly?

Roll one end of a paper over a pencil. Blow over the top. How does moving air help lift a bird up in the air?

Blow up a balloon. Drop it and an empty one at the same time. How do air sacs help birds fly?

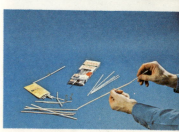

Balance 5 red straws with 5 blue ones. Fill the red ones with pipe cleaners. Balance again. How would bones filled with air help a bird?

Some birds cannot fly.
These birds have wings,
but they do not use their
wings to fly.

kiwi

ostrich

emu

penguins

This bird does not use its wings to fly.
It uses its wings to move in the water.

SOUTH FOR THE WINTER

In the winter the air is cold.
The ground is cold, too.
Some birds cannot find enough food to eat.
They must go where it is warm.
They must go where there is food.
The birds will fly away to the south.

Some birds fly in the day, and rest
and eat at night.
Other birds fly at night.
Most birds use flyways.
Flyways are like roads in the air.

Pacific Flyway

Central Flyway

Mississippi Flyway

Atlantic Flyway

Some birds fly south in groups called flocks.
Other birds fly in a V-shaped group.

Sometimes it is wet and cold.

A few birds may get lost, but these birds have found their way.

They are where it is warm.

The birds find food in the warm ground.

When spring comes, the birds will fly back north and lay their eggs.

PICTURE DICTIONARY

A bird's **CROP** helps grind up hard foods such as seeds. After the food is softer, it goes to the stomach.

A large number of birds that stay or fly together is called a **FLOCK.**

A **FLYWAY** is like a path birds follow each year as they fly south in winter, or as they come back north in the spring.

MUSCLES are strong parts in the bodies of animals and people. They help the body move and do work.

In a bird, **SACS** are like little bags that can be filled with air. They help keep the bird cool.

The reading vocabulary of this book is at the second grade level.

ACKNOWLEDGMENTS

Illustrations: James Teason
Lucy and John Hawkinson

Photos: William R. Eastman/ Tom Stack and Associates (page 4)
Photography Unlimited (pages 1, 21, 41)

Cover: Norman Herlihy (design)
Product Illustration, Inc. (art work)

Demonstration found on page 37.
Experiments found on pages 21 and 41.
Detailed explanation of these experiments available in the filmstrips **Finding Out About Birds: Experiment 1** and **Finding Out About Birds: Experiment 2.**